Design David West
Children's Book Design
Editor Margaret Fagan
Picture researcher Cecilia Weston-Baker

The author, Elizabeth Hoddes, works for The Stepfamilies Association, Cambridge. She is the author of several books and articles about stepfamilies.

© Aladdin Books 1990

First published in
the United States in 1990 by
Gloucester Press
387 Park Avenue South
New York NY 10016

Printed in Belgium

The publishers wish to acknowledge that the photographs reproduced in this book have been posed by models or obtained from photographic agencies.

ISBN 0-531-17226-0

Library of Congress Catalog
Card No: 89 81611

# CONTENTS

# UNDERSTANDING SOCIAL ISSUES

# STEPFAMILIES

## Elizabeth Hodder

# GLOUCESTER PRESS

New York : London : Toronto : Sydney

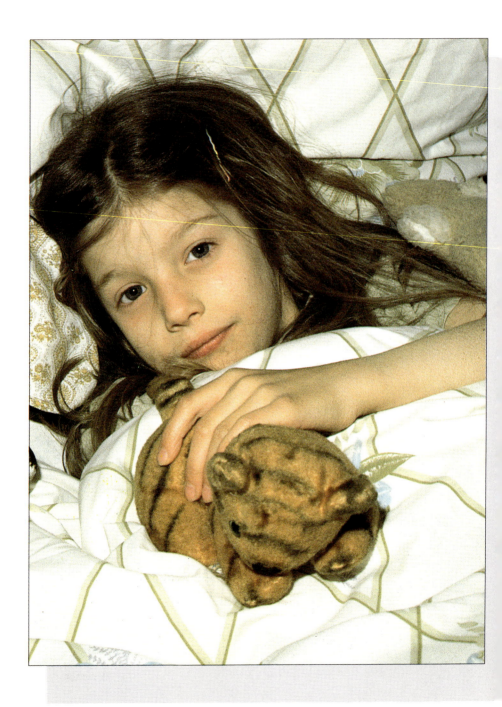

Most people have a negative stereotype of a stepfamily which they may have learnt at an early age from fairy stories. They imagine the family consists of a wicked stepparent, an ideal "real" parent and an innocent child. As with all fairy stories there is a grain of truth in some of this: real-life stepparents can occasionally be mean. But then, who isn't sometimes? And are step-children always likely to be sweet-tempered and treated badly?

Unlike divorced families or widowed families, stepfamilies are not easy to pick out or recognize; they are often confused with other types of family, such as foster-families or extended families. They have been somewhat ignored in the past because only a small percentage of the population was thought to be involved. Now, however, the step-family is an increasingly common type of family and its social importance is considerable.

Society can no longer ignore the stepfamily, treating it as some kind of abnormal family type. Whether formed after death (formerly the major reason why a stepfamily was created) or after divorce (now by far the most usual event preceding the creation of a stepfamily), there is no doubt that the stepfamily is very common today. Some analyses suggest that it will be the most numerous single form of family by the beginning of the twenty-first century. We therefore need to know what a stepfamily is, what its main problems are, what effects it can have on both parents and children, and why it is a major social issue requiring more understanding and acceptance.

**Many of the old fairy stories told to children at bedtime give an unpleasant and unhappy picture of stepfamily life.**

## CHAPTER 1

# HISTORY AND BACKGROUND OF THE STEPFAMILY

The death of a parent used to be the main reason for stepfamilies. Today most stepfamilies are created after divorce.

Stepfamilies have always been with us and probably always will be. In the past, inevitably, many stepfamilies were created after death. Life expectancy was much lower than it is today. The burdens of childbirth, the many fatal diseases and the greater likelihood of death from violent causes meant that many families in the past expected at least one parent not to survive even into middle age. It was not uncommon to find a family of children with just one natural, or biological, parent; and a new parent – a stepparent – would be found to "step" in to help bring up the children. Sometimes this would take the form of a commercial transaction, or perhaps a marriage of convenience, with a widower and his children marrying a spinster – or even a widow with children herself.

**Parental roles**
In the past, too, the roles of parents were much more clearly defined: the woman to be wife and mother and the man to be the breadwinner and disciplinarian. It was unlikely that such stepfamilies would be based on love between the partners or between the parents and children. But this does not necessarily mean that such families were unsuccessful. They need to be judged against the "normal" family life at that time, which was often harsh and focused primarily on survival.

Elsewhere in the world, stepfamilies have sometimes resulted from the prevailing cultural and religious beliefs. In some Muslim countries, for instance, a man may take more than one wife – up to four if he wishes and is able to afford them.

This means that the children may be brought up by stepmothers as well as by their own natural mothers.

**Stepfamilies and divorce**

It is only in recent years that stepfamilies have become primarily associated with the rising divorce rates in both Britain and the United States. It is not true, however, that the bad image which society gives stepfamilies, and which they therefore give themselves, is simply the result of the bad image of divorce. The bad image of stepfamilies was there long before and the post-divorce stepfamily is merely confirming that image. But why have stepfamilies always had this negative image? And where do the fairy tale myths about wicked stepmothers and cruel stepfathers come from?

Steprelations are often many and complex in Muslim families because a man is allowed to take more than one wife.

Sometimes it is the father who has to cope with bringing up a child alone.

## Death

We all nurse mixed emotions and even hypocritical attitudes about death. On the one hand we are naturally very sympathetic to the grieving parent on the loss of his or her partner, but if not. enough time appears to be taken over the grieving process before they take another partner, we can become extremely angry. We see the new marriage as a betrayal of the dead husband or wife. And if the new partner happens to be younger and more attractive than the original partner then we can become very hostile indeed. In such circumstances, unfavorable comments are made: "He has never considered the children," or "She is only marrying him for his looks/money." But such unfair criticisms are rarely made of a first marriage. And people entering into this kind of new stepfamily are likely to be made aware very soon

that those around them are unwelcoming. As a result, they may behave in a very negative way, particularly toward the children, thereby confirming the negative opinions of others.

**The grieving process after a death can be long and very painful.**

## Wicked stepmothers and stepfathers

In the past, life was often harsh and unloving in many families. Children were often thought of as a means of providing support for the family and were expected to be tough. The parents were often hard taskmasters, handing out more discipline than love, usually because they had to in order to survive. The mother was overworked and tired, with little patience for the needs of her children. But this picture was too unpleasant for most people to want to read about, nurturing as they did the idealistic vision of caring parents and doting children. In order to cope with this contrast between the unpleasant reality of the real-life mother and the idealized mother of their imaginations, they invented the stepmother. She, the stepmother, could take on all the horrible characteristics of the real-life mother, relieving all readers from any conflict. Unfortunately, we have come to believe the fairy tales over the years. This makes it much more difficult for stepparents and stepchildren to be relaxed about their stepfamilies.

> **"My Dad used to give me a cuddle in the evening, but now my stepmom watches him all the time. She's down on him like a ton of bricks if he so much as smiles at me." Sharon, aged 14**

**Money matters**
Because stepfamilies are generally preceded by a period of upheaval, it is quite usual for their financial positions to be precarious. The whole matter of maintenance payments for the children can add considerably to other pressures within a stepfamily. Even more difficult is the common case where the second wife has to go out to work to help meet the payments her husband has to pay his ex-wife. Money is often used as a weapon in stepfamilies and it may also be used as a means of compensating both adults and children for something that happened in the past. With many more mouths to feed, stepfamilies often face major financial difficulties. These difficulties may coincide with housing, employment and legal problems; and quite often stepfamilies may have to start all over again in buying a house or finding a new career.

## A happy ending?

Despite the financial and emotional strains faced by some stepfamiles, many eventually do evolve so that matters of money and relationships are dealt with to everyone's satisfaction. Peter, who is 16, lives with his father, stepmother, and her two children, and likes having two new younger sisters.

**Stepdaughter-stepmother relationships are often particularly difficult and can lead to a great deal of tension within the stepfamily.**

# CHAPTER 2

# WHAT DO WE MEAN BY A STEPFAMILY?

> Because all the children in a stepfamily are not from the same parents, they may not look like each other.

According to sections of the press and some of the stories we read, the stepfamily is a lesser kind of family in which adults who have ruined their first marriages decide to try again, this time with their (reluctant and resentful) children in tow. Such a chaotic sequence of events is a launching pad for some stepfamilies, but a far greater number are well planned and carefully thought out. Unlike the traditional nuclear family – the one endlessly portrayed by advertisers – the stepfamily does not have a clear, uniform background common to all its members. In fact there are many different types of stepfamily, depending on the variety of backgrounds of its members and the new patterns of life to follow (full-time or part-time, for example).

## How to define a stepfamily

A stepfamily is created when one or both of the new adult partners brings a child or children from a previous relationship to the new family. The key facts are that a stepfamily has ready-made children, either young or old, full-time or part-time. Legally speaking, a stepfamily only exists where the partners are married, but conventionally – and for the purposes of this book – a stepfamily does not have to follow a previous marriage; nor does it require a marriage to confirm its status as a stepfamily. Many stepfamilies today involve adults and children living together, either full-time or part-time.

**Many families join together to celebrate when mom or dad remarries. They welcome the new stepmother and accept the challenge of getting to know new siblings.**

## The post-divorce stepfamily

This is perhaps the most common type of step-

family. It may involve a mother and her children living with/marrying a partner who is not the father of her children. He thus becomes the children's stepfather. The children's natural father (now divorced from their mother) may still see his children regularly under access arrangements. But he, too, may take a new partner – perhaps also a woman with children of her own. So he becomes a stepfather. He is at the same time father to his own children (to whom he has regular access) and stepfather to his new wife's children. His new wife is mother to her own children and part-time stepmother to her husband's children when they come to visit. Her children and her stepchildren become stepbrothers/stepsisters and stepchildren. And this is a relatively simple example!

> **"I'm just appalled at the way my stepdad lets his kids walk all over him at weekends. They just have to ask for some allowance or some new sneakers and he gives it to them. He spoils them rotten."**
> **Simon, aged 15**

### The post-widowhood stepfamily

This was the normal road to stepfamilyhood before divorce took its toll on the nuclear family. A widow or widower, having lost her or his partner, then takes on a new partner to become stepmother/ stepfather to the children. If the new partner has not previously been in a family unit, there will be few problems of access, ex-wives or ex-husbands in the background, at least in theory. In practice, however, a stepfamily formed after death

can be as difficult as one formed after divorce. It is sometimes the memory of the dead parent that can destroy the stepfamily. Jealousy, guilt and many other powerful emotions can take their toll just as much – sometimes more so – even though the object of that emotion is no longer alive.

Under access arrangements the father can still see his child regularly. This can be difficult, but it is very much in the child's best interests that access should be taken up.

> "I just wish the kids were less fussy about their food. Whatever I cook for them they object to. They are always telling me what a wonderful cook their mother was. I have to stop myself from reminding them that their mother is dead and if it wasn't for me they'd be starving. I get so mad."
> Mrs S., newly remarried

### The "single-parent and child" stepfamily
This kind of stepfamily occurs when a woman has

deliberately chosen to have a child or children outside any kind of permanent relationship, but then decides to take a partner to live with or marry. On the surface this would seem to be a simple situation, but in practice it is filled with exactly the same kinds of problems faced by other types of stepfamilies. And, as far as its acceptance by society is concerned, this form of stepfamily has the additional stigma of illegitimacy or "single-parent family" to cope with. Each of these types of stepfamily, and the many other types that exist, has its own unique characteristics as well as common features and problems.

## The stepfamily in society

To some extent the stepfamily is largely invisible. It is rarely possible to look at a family in a doctor's waiting room or playing in a park and say "Yes, that's a stepfamily." To an outsider a stepfamily may look like any other family, even though there may be clear physical differences between the children and adults as well as unusually wide differences in ages. But this invisibility is partly the result of the stepfamily's own desire to "keep a low profile." Those involved may feel ashamed about their pasts – the adults may feel very guilty about the harm they have done to their children, and the children may be anxious that their family should not be seen to be different from those of their friends. Whatever the reason, stepfamilies are very good at maintaining a low profile, often pretending they are a "normal" nuclear family – perhaps even changing their surnames to ensure that an outsider cannot guess their secret. Part of

The "one-parent family" unit is becoming more common and more accepted. If the mother then takes on a partner, a particular type of stepfamily will be formed.

**Adult couples who form the basis of stepfamilies are often "invisible" in that they cannot easily be identified as members of a stepfamily by just looking at them.**

this secrecy results from the poor image which stepfamilies have. Many of the more sensational stories in the media about child abuse, for instance, seem to involve stepfamilies. While there is no hard evidence to support the opinion that child abuse is more likely to occur in a stepfamily, it is an assumption that is widely held and can even influence society's view of the stepfamily.

## Second-best families?

It is hardly surprising, then, that stepparents feel society is critical of them, perhaps even regarding them as second-best, less warm and affectionate, less kind and generally less stable and competent than nuclear families. But, as we noted earlier, many stepparents are also natural parents, either to their own children from a previous relationship or to new children of the new relationship. Unfor-

tunately, because of the conviction that step-parents are not valued, they are sometimes less likely to seek help when problems and difficulties arise. They are worried that others will assume that they have problems because a stepparent is a "lesser" parent. For children, too, the prospect of a new stepparent can sound alarm bells which may lead them to hold back or behave badly to save them from getting hurt.

**It is not possible to look at any group in a playing field and say "That is a stepfamily." Stepfamilies are not easily identifiable.**

## Stepfamily statistics
There are very few statistics about stepfamilies – partly because of their desire for invisibility, partly because of the difficulty of defining a stepfamily for statistical purposes, and partly because census returns do not include questions on stepfamilies. But the situation is improving and before long we should have a much more precise set of

**Stepparents are often very reluctant to seek help from a family doctor or other sources because they feel society disapproves of them and often undervalues them.**

figures to study. At the moment it is commonly accepted that there are at least 6 million members of stepfamilies in Britain. This number is increasing as one in three first marriages ends in divorce; the figure is one in two for second marriages. In some schools at least one third – in some cases over a half – of the pupils are in some form of stepfamily. Clearly the numbers of people in stepfamilies are great and substantially underestimated in the available figures. Thus, it is possible that by the end of this century the stepfamily, defined in its broadest sense, may well become the most common single family type in Britain.

The same is true of the United States, where statistics are probably more reliable. It has recently been officially stated there that there are 35 million stepparents in the country and that there are 1,300 stepfamilies formed every day. At least

one in five children has a stepparent. These figures are staggering enough, but they do not take account of the increasing trend for partners and parents to cohabit rather than marry. One in four children born today in Britain is "illegitimate," though this is not to say that such children do not have stable and happy homes. The stigma of illegitimacy, like stepfamilyhood, is beginning to weaken, though we still have a long way to go in ensuring that children born outside of marriage are fully accepted by society.

Whether we take the figures relating to legally defined stepfamilies or those estimates relating to all kinds of stepfamilies, including cohabitation, there is no doubt that numbers are increasing and are likely to go on increasing. This is not a moral judgment: it is a fact, and society has to face up to the implications of that fact.

**Stepfamilies can be successful, with a great deal of love and warmth developing between the stepparent and stepchild.**

"I think that the law about being a step-parent should be changed. As I see it I have no responsibilities. Legally it seems as if I could get nothing at all out of the years I've spent trying to be a good stepmother." Mrs T., New York

Even without hard statistical facts, some very clear trends emerge. It appears, for example, that widows are less likely to remarry than divorced women; and it is possible to offer a number of reasons for this. Likewise, it is much more likely that younger women (widowed or divorced) will remarry. In the United States, three out of five divorced women under 40 will remarry within two years, but the number drops dramatically after that age. The obvious explanation for this is that younger women are more likely to be attractive to men, but it may also be that the younger we are the more flexible and adaptable we are.

Men show roughly the same trends as women, but they usually remarry younger women. Moreover, while the rate of remarriage for men under 40 in the United States is very high – four out of five – the rate does not decline so clearly after 40. As in the United Kingdom, there is a pool of older divorced and widowed women.

Stepfamilies are notoriously unstable, with a divorce rate for second marriages of one in two in the United Kingdom and almost three in five in the United States. Unlike in first marriages, where the most commonly quoted reasons for the breakdown are sexual incompatability and an inability to communicate, in stepfamilies it is the inability of one

partner to get on with the other partner's children.

> **"I just wish my wife would be a bit more forthcoming with my children. She treats them so coldly, as if she hates them. She never shows any warmth. They think it's something they've done to offend her."**
> **Mr W.**

**Any happy group of children may well include those whose parents are divorced or cohabiting. And some of the children may be born outside of marriage or from one-parent families.**

Numerically, there are more stepfathers than stepmothers. Many stepfathers may well feel a sense of failure as a natural father. For the majority of stepfathers *are* also natural fathers, though most of them do not live with their own children. This can arouse feelings of hostility toward the step-children with whom they have to live. These children are a constant reminder of their own children from whom they have been separated.

# CASE STUDY

Sharon and Bob have just gotten married – both for the second time. Sharon is 31 and Bob is quite a bit older at 44. Sharon is divorced and has custody of her two sons, Jonathan (aged eight) and Simon (aged three). Bob is also divorced, but his two children live with his ex-wife, visiting Sharon and Bob at weekends. They are both teenagers. The older one, Tina, is 17 and the younger one, Mark, is 13.

As Sharon says, everything has been turned upside down by their new marriage. "I'd no idea how complicated it was going to be. I thought everything would just settle down and we would become one big happy family. But so far that hasn't happened." For Bob there has been quite an adjustment to make. "Being that much older than Sharon I'd become accustomed to teenage children. OK, they are more difficult in some ways, but at least they go out some of the time and in any case they only come at weekends. Sharon's children, being so young, seem to be around all the time. It's the noise I can't get used to."

Sharon is very conscious of Bob's misgivings about her children. "I try to keep them quiet when he gets home from work in the evenings. After all, they are not his children and I know he misses his own children quite a lot. But you know what it's like with children. The more you try to quiet them down, the more rebellious and noisy they seem to become. Bob's very good. He never loses his temper, but he doesn't seem to be getting any closer to them."

"Of course the worst time is at weekends when his two teenagers come over. They have to have separate bedrooms. So that means that Jonathan and Simon have to come and sleep in our bedroom. You can imagine what that does for our privacy! No one is to blame for the situation, but it does try your patience. Sometimes by the end of a weekend I feel quite frazzled, what with trying to keep my two children quiet and also trying to do interesting things with Bob's children, who always seem to be bored by us, anyway. I suppose it will get better."

Bob is equally confused by what is happening. "I do feel

very guilty about my own two children – what damage the divorce has done to them and how I've destroyed their family life. And in a way that holds me back and stops me from making this new family work. Sharon would like us to have a baby of our own. She thinks that would help us all to feel like a committed family. Frankly, the thought terrifies me."

## CASE STUDY 2

Problems caused by age gaps can show themselves in many different ways. When older children are faced with the birth of a new baby in the stepfamily, they can feel excluded and resentful.

Angie's father recently got married again to his young secretary, Linda. Angie used to call in to see her Dad after school or when she was passing with her friends. Her Dad always seemed to be pleased to see her. "But not any more. He goes quiet and starts to look shifty – you know, as if he's got something to hide from me. And he has, really, because he got Linda pregnant and then she got him to marry

her. I just think it's all disgusting. After all, he's nearly 40 now and he's already gone through that babies and nappies bit."

Angie's father was divorced by her mother two years ago when Angie was 14. For the last two years she has been living with her mother and young brother, Jason, in the house they have always lived in. Her Dad moved out into a tiny modern apartment and now lives there with Linda. The new baby is expected any day.

"I feel so sad. He's my Dad and when Mom and I have our arguments, which is almost every day, I need to know that Dad is there to turn to. Well he isn't any more. He doesn't need me. He's got his new wife and soon he'll have a new baby and he'll forget all about me. Instead of being happy to see me, I'm just a constant reminder of his awful marriage to Mom. I can't talk to him any more. And as for Linda, well she just wants me out of the way so she can get to work on Dad and turn him against his family for good. It's not fair. I love my Dad but I think he's already stopped loving me."

## CHAPTER 3

# ARE STEPFAMILIES DIFFERENT ?

Though many
stepfamilies may
look like other
families, they are
different in some
important
respects and
these differences
can cause severe
tensions among
stepfamily
members.

Most people carry around an idea of the perfect family. Such a family is set up after a happy, romantic courtship and marriage in a church or temple. After a suitable time lapse babies appear to complete the home and family and the partners stay together "till death us do part." Pain, misery, selfishness and greed are not part of the "ideal" family. If there are any arguments they take place between other people – not between the "ideal" couple. Of course no family is ever really like this, since most people are a mixture of good and bad; and it is only within the family that these two opposing sides of our nature can surface, day after day.

## Stepfamilies and conflict

Within a stepfamily it is probably true that the conflict between the good and the bad is more likely to surface – in both adults and children. A stepfamily arouses very strong feelings in its members, partly because of what has happened in the past and because its members do not all have a common history. Sometimes one or more members of a stepfamily cannot cope with their feelings, and try to blame others for what seems to be going wrong in their lives.

"I just can't get along with my stepson – everything about him irritates me, like the way he talks, eats, runs. He only wants his Dad, Mom and Nanna and he thinks I caused his Mom to go away, which isn't true." Mrs A

At other times, people may deny having these

these feelings altogether. So it is worth looking at some of the features that characterize stepfamilies and may lead to the rise of very specific problems.

## Second time around

Stepfamilies are created the "second time around." This means that everyone – adults and children – has experience of a previous family of some kind

Children helping in the home is part of the picture we have of the normal, happy home – the kind of home most stepfamilies share or wish for.

**It is sometimes very difficult to cope with the stresses of living in a stepfamily.**

and may find it more difficult to adjust to a new regime with different rules and different habits. When two families combine under one roof they cannot continue to live as they did before – at least one person has to give up cherished customs such as the times of meals, bedtimes, the amount of television to be watched and so on. That sounds much easier than it is, as most of us get much of our security from doing things the same way each day. When change is insisted upon we may feel threatened and become negative in our behavior.

### Loss

Many stepfamily members suffer from a sense of loss through death or divorce of a partner or parent. They may or may not have been able to show their grief and may be at different levels of acceptance of the replacement partner or parent.

When we lose someone dear to us – even if it is as the result of a bitter divorce – we are changed. If the loss is not acknowledged, or is denied, then we can become scarred emotionally and that affects the way we approach living in a stepfamily.

## The past

Because the stepfamily is "a second time around family" it involves commitments and memories which are not necessarily shared by all its members. This can arouse feelings of insecurity and jealousy in both adults and children. When they have to listen to stories about happy family holidays with someone else, for example, a partner may start dwelling on his or her partner's previous sexual relations. The lack of a shared past or shared memories can accentuate the stepfamily's feelings of being different.

A group of teenage stepchildren who know at firsthand what it is like trying to combine two families under one roof.

## So many people

We all live with the expectation of having just two parents, and it can come as quite a shock to children when they find they have three, four, or even more. Then, of course, there are all the new relatives, especially stepgrandparents, they may acquire. Suddenly to acquire new relatives and to have no rules about how to treat them can lead to feelings of inadequacy and guilt. For children the dilemma is one of divided loyalties. Is it right to extend their affection and love to new parents and relatives without feeling that their natural parents are being betrayed, for example? It is also possible that problems will arise when new sets of relatives and grandparents do not get along with each other or with the children. Stepfamily life may, more than in nuclear families, require everyone to have the capacity to get along with others, some of whom they may not like at all, and in a manner not expected in nuclear families.

> "My friends say I am really lucky with my stepmom. I suppose she's young and quite good-looking. But I just wish I was with my own Mom. But she doesn't want me living with her because she's got a new boyfriend." Julie, recently moved to live with her new stepfamily

## Ready-made personalities

This may seem rather obvious, but in the case of the children in a stepfamily it is an important distinguishing feature. Most children's personalities are shaped early in their lives, either

through genetic traits or through environmental factors; which is the more important is a matter of some debate. When children become members of a new family where the genetic links and environmental factors are very different, a new family is suddenly formed. This usually occurs without the slow, gradual process of parents and children interacting over the years. One aggrieved stepparent described this experience as "looking after a Martian who has escaped from the moon and desperately wants to go back." Having ready-made personalities increases the possibility of conflict for both parents and children in a stepfamily. The parent sees little point in trying when the stepchildren are going to turn out just the same whatever they do. And the stepchildren can feel lonely and isolated when trying to adapt to a very strange and different new parent.

**Grandparents need not be deprived of the joy of seeing their grandchildren when the parents divorce and remarry. Grandchildren and stepgrandchildren can be loved and helped in many ways.**

## Chaos and visiting

Chaos reigns in most families at times, but perhaps it is more likely to be prevalent in stepfamilies. Often chaos is not of their own making, but occurs as they try to reestablish family boundaries out of the mess from the past. Some of the chaos revolves around the problem of children who are expected nevertheless to make regular visits at weekends to see their other natural parent; sometimes this is arranged at the expense of being with their friends or pursuing their own hobbies in their own homes. Children often dislike this enforced decamping, feeling resentment toward adults who are preventing them from leading a normal life. Adults in stepfamilies also often dislike the dominance of ex-wives or ex-husbands who appear to exercise considerable influence over how the stepfamily operates, constantly adding to the chaos by making new demands, either emotional or financial – or both.

## Feeling different

The sense of disorder and chaos adds to the general feeling of being different, and that worries many members of stepfamilies. For some adults this feeling can lead them to behave in ways that are not always appropriate to the situation. Sometimes there is a strong desire to blot out the past and to pretend they live in a nuclear family with no hint of death or divorce behind them. They may refuse to allow the children weekend access to their natural parent, for example; or they may adopt the same surname, or move house – all as part of an attempt to hide their background.

Alternatively, they may convince themselves that their former background is something to be ashamed of. This may result in a refusal to talk about their problems, either to each other, or to those outside the family, making it more likely that such problems will become entrenched.

Even the bonds between a mother and her son can be threatened by jealousy over a new stepfather or stepbrother in the home.

## Relationships between the children

Children may suddenly find themselves coping with a whole new set of stepbrothers and step-sisters as a family is formed. They may view these new siblings as rivals for their parents' attention. If, on the other hand, the children feel sure enough of their parents' love, then they may well find it easier to accept these new stepbrothers and stepsisters. Inevitably there will be disagreements because the "new" children will have different habits, some of which can be particularly annoying. Also, if children feel that one or more of them is being spoilt, then this can cause serious feelings of jealousy. Such a situation is common when one or more children go away at weekends to see their mother or father and then return with new clothes, presents and money. The children left behind can feel badly treated and may seek revenge in one way or another.

Finally, a stepfamily's distinguishing features can be looked at from the point of view which regards family life as part of a cycle. Our previously clear understanding of what a family is, how it originates and what its relationships should be are upset by the stepfamily. For the stepfamily interrupts the normal cycle and is a family without clear boundaries. It has what may be viewed as untidy origins and may be untidy in appearance. It is often wrongly judged as a result.

Parents in a stepfamily may need to talk with the teacher about such matters as the child having a new or different surname when the stepfamily is formed.

# CASE STUDY

Donna had a baby boy (Les) when she was 18 and for a while she lived with her parents who took care of the baby while she went to work. This worked quite well for a time until her child began to be too much of a handful for her parents to manage. So Donna and Les moved into their own apartment.

In the apartment underneath Donna's there lived a father and two young children. The mother had been killed in a car accident. Donna soon saw that she and the father downstairs could make life easier for themselves: "Steve works shifts at the local car factory and it was really difficult for him to manage the day-to-day problems like shopping and cooking and picking the children up from school. Somehow I just seemed to be there and offered to help.

Well, things just went on from there. One minute I was cooking supper for his children and the next minute we were getting a babysitter for all three children. We began to spend quite a lot of time together. We got along well and soon decided to get a bigger apartment for all five of us to live in together. So far it's working out quite well, though we do have big disagreements about the children. Steve is just so easy on his kids. I suppose he wants to make it up to them for losing their mother, though the car accident wasn't his fault – she was driving alone at the time. But whatever they ask for he gives them: candy, toys, clothes – he is forever buying them things. Perhaps it's because Les and I had a tough time early on that I feel resentful. But I just can't bear to see his children spoiled that way. And of course Les notices that the other two children are always getting new things.

Yes, we have big arguments about it and always at the end of them I feel just like a wicked stepmother being cruel and spiteful to her stepchildren. It's not that I'm jealous or don't like his kids. I just think he's spoiling them so badly that when they get older they'll treat him like dirt. I want Les to treat me with respect when he grows up. I don't want to be trampled all over by my kid or anyone else's. It's a shame, but I can see us splitting up over it all. If only he didn't have children, it would be great."

**CHAPTER 4**

# PROBLEMS BETWEEN STEPPARENT AND STEPCHILD

Children in most
stepfamilies have
special problems
to cope with and
can easily feel
rejected and
alone.

Just looking at the background to the formation of a stepfamily gives us a good indication of why there are often problems between stepparents and stepchildren. The incoming parent immediately creates a triangular relationship, coming between the stepchild and its absent natural parent. Everyone in the family has different hopes and fears. Some of the problems arise because of the contrasting expectations of the adults and children in a stepfamily.

## Expectations and difficulties

When parents lose their partner through death or divorce, it is a natural instinct to try to replace that partner, partly for love and companionship and partly to replace the children's missing parent. It is often assumed that the children will go along with this. Unfortunately, this is seldom the case.

Children often have a different view of their parents' needs and functions. Many children consider that a parent is there largely to serve his or her own needs and therefore has few, if any, selfish desires such as the need to seek love and companionship from another adult. When the parent does just that the child may feel considerable rejection, as the adult appears to be seeking a new partner in preference to the child.

In such an atmosphere, a child may be unwilling to view the new stepparent as anything other than a rival: someone who has taken away their one remaining parent and who should be gotten rid of as soon as possible. Otherwise the child may feel that their surviving natural parent might be lost to them forever.

"When my new dad came I didn't like him. I remember thinking that there wasn't really room for my mom, me, and him. I used to ask my mom when he was going back to his own house." Alice, aged 12

Even the natural mother may have little idea of the thoughts and feelings her child has about being in a stepfamily.

The natural parent may have no idea of what the child is thinking and will, for all the best motives, try to make the relationship between the new partner (stepparent) and child close and friendly. This often confirms in the child's eyes the fact that the parent undoubtedly prefers the new adult and that the child is being pushed to one side. A new stepparent may be aware of this rejection by the stepchild, but is often unable to be sympathetic or forgiving. Rather, they take the rejection personally and begin a process of fault-finding and retaliation, so living up to their unpleasant "wicked" image. None of us likes rejection, but it is especially difficult to accept when you have done nothing to deserve it. In the eyes of many, though not all, stepparents, their motives are unquestionably to be a good and kind parent to the new ready-made families, and they are unable to cope with the hostility their presence arouses. It is easy to see how such a situation can degenerate into all-out war, with stepparent and stepchild determined to dislike one another.

> **"When my ex-husband comes to pick up the children for the weekend my husband goes upstairs so he can scowl at him from the bedroom window. You can cut the atmosphere with a knife." Mrs T.**

Even the smallest effort to understand the other's point of view can help put matters in perspective. This requires time and the support of other people, and frequently these are not available to the stepfamily. On top of this there are other problems for both adults and children in a stepfamily, making it more difficult for all con-

cerned to bridge the gap in communication.

## Jealousy

Seldom does a day pass without many of us feeling pangs of jealousy of one kind or another. Perhaps a friend has done well in a competition or a boyfriend shows a passing interest in another girl. Such events can make us feel insecure. Our self-confidence evaporates and all of a sudden we are eaten up by jealousy. In a stepfamily almost everyone is insecure for a while – adults and children alike – with the result that they are all prone to bouts of jealous behavior, whether or not they will admit it!

## Adult jealousy

Adults are as capable of jealousy as children. In a stepfamily the new stepparent is almost certainly

**Jealousy is a particularly frequent cause of arguments between partners in a stepfamily.**

jealous of their partner's children; sometimes this jealousy takes the form of being highly critical and vindictive, occasionally toward only one child. Such behavior seems more common between individuals of the same sex – between a stepmother and stepdaughter and between a stepfather and his stepson.

> "My stepdaughter is only seven, but she's a real minx. If she comes in the sitting room and finds me sitting by my husband watching television she immediately sits down between us, forcing us apart. I know she does it on purpose, and it makes me mad. But all my husband does is just smile and put his arm around her." Mrs M.

In some instances the jealousy may be the result of the child's manner and appearance, which happens to be very similar to the manner and appearance of the partner's previous husband or wife. Thus it is a form of sexual jealousy: the stepparent is jealous of the partner's previous sexual relationship and the particular child in question is just a daily reminder of this earlier sexual partner. Such irrational thinking on the part of the stepparent is often vigorously denied. Excuses will be found for singling out a particular child for criticism and disciplining, since the truth is often too difficult to live with.

### Insecure stepparents
Insecure stepparents are also prone to other forms of jealousy. They may be jealous of the secure

relationship between their partner and his/her children. Because it is so close and loving it can make the stepparent feel excluded, left on the outside and fighting to establish a role. It is unlikely that the natural parent will be aware of the jealousy coming from his partner or that he/she could moderate his/her behavior. Stepparents may also display jealousy toward the ex-husband or ex-wife, especially if the presence of the latter makes itself felt in the new stepfamily.

The stepparent is always aware of the pressure put on him to love his new stepchild as if the child was his own.

"I really have tried to cope with my feelings toward his previous partner. They lived together for so many years and then she died. In the end I went to see a counselor because I knew these feelings were spoiling our everyday life together. I think I was living more in the past than David was." Helen, partner to David

For an insecure stepparent, the idea of the previous wife or husband exercising a continuing and powerful influence over what is now his or her own family is too difficult to accept. They would rather this "ex" would really become an "ex" and disappear altogether. A lot of energy can be expended by both partners, and in many cases the energy would be better spent on trying to build up the strength of the stepfamily.

## Children's jealousy

Children's jealousy is equally destructive. For those children who are still feeling battered and bruised as a result of a divorce or the death of their parent, the appearance of any new adult on the scene is likely to provoke a strong, jealous response. In the child's eyes, the new adult is there primarily to take their mom or dad away from them. Their strong feelings of jealousy may pro-

Stepchildren can feel excluded and unable to take part spontaneously in stepfamily life. They can easily become withdrawn and oversensitive.

voke uncharacteristic forms of behavior – alternately seeking attention and being very withdrawn. They may go back to early childlike behavior – bed-wetting, truanting, stealing or being destructive at school, leading teachers and other adults to express concern about the child. Some of this concern may take the form of condemnation of the stepparent: "The child was all right until she got a new stepmom." In one sense this is true. However, for a jealous child to feel loved and accepted and not under threat from another adult demands considerable tolerance from everyone – their natural parents, and especially the two adults concerned.

## Loving everyone in the family – or not!

A key problem area for stepfamilies is the question of living with people you don't love or even like. It is true that we may not always love our parents, brothers or sisters in a nuclear family – especially from time to time. In fact, in conventional families parents, brothers and sisters are often taken for granted, becoming just "part of the wallpaper." In a sense, therefore, it is easy to ask: "Well, does it matter if stepparents and stepchildren do not love each other?" The answer is it certainly seems to matter to most stepparents and stepchildren.

"It's not so bad being in a stepfamily when things are going well, but when they're going badly it's much worse because there's no one to talk to like there used to be." Mandy, aged 11

### Role of the natural parent

The natural parent is the key element to acceptance, or otherwise, of a non-loving relationship between the stepparent and stepchildren. The stepparent will be aware of the pressure to love his/her stepchildren. But the greater the pressure the more resentment it yields. In a sense there is no reason why the new stepparent should love his/her stepchildren. For a stepmother to love a child's natural father does not mean that she will immediately – or ever – love his child. It may be that love comes in time. Or it may be that love never comes. Many people seem to expect – even demand – instant love.

### Hate – the opposite of love?

Children are faced with similar problems. Their reaction to not loving their stepparent ( or new stepbrothers or sisters) can often result in their believing that above all else they really hate them. The simple opposite of love seems to be hate. Children feel uncomfortable having a new and strange adult around whose habits are alien and who starts to take control of their lives. To hate them is a way of coping. Being able to accept some "halfway" house, something between loving and hating, is often very difficult. This is particularly true for teenagers.

> "Once my stepdad started telling me what time I should be in at night I told him – 'that's it, I'm leaving.' I told him that only my real Dad can tell me what to do. Then I walked out." Jason, aged 16

Some children find they simply cannot get on with their new "siblings" and may feel the situation unbearable. Perhaps there are huge age gaps between them if their respective parents had children at different stages in their lives. But the arrival of new siblings can have other effects. Suddenly there may be friends of the same age in the family, or, occasionally, strong sexual feelings between siblings.

## Guilt

Another very strong and dominating emotion in the behavior of stepfamilies is guilt. It is not confined to the adults. The trouble with guilt is that – like jealousy – it is an irrational, but very destructive, emotion.

> **"I hate going to my daughter's school on social occasions. She still keeps my former married name and you can see the teachers looking at me when they find my surname is not the same as my daughter's." Mrs H.**

For adults, guilt in a stepfamily usually stems from their experiences in the past. Their behavior in the stepfamily is often based on a need to compensate, or make up, for the past. Sometimes they seek to compensate for what they see as their own bad behavior. For example, they may have walked out on their first spouse and children, and feel ashamed of this – even if the situation had been intolerable. Or they may seek to compensate for something that they had no control over, such as the death of a partner. For whatever reason, guilt produces uncontrollable behavior. There are numerous examples: the father who only sees his children one weekend a month and for those two days spoils them and ignores his wife and his new baby; the widow who fusses around her young son, ignoring her new husband. Because guilt is the motivator, those concerned are unreceptive to reasonable discussion. They seem locked into behavior patterns which they are powerless to change. The pressure this puts on some stepfamilies is considerable.

### How could it have been your fault?

Children, too, are often driven by guilt in stepfamilies – guilt that they could have been the cause of their parents' divorce; guilt that they might have been responsible for their parent's death in some strange way; guilt that it is wrong to like, let alone love, their stepparent; guilt that their absent parent is unhappy. Such guilt-ridden behavior can sadly add to a child's confusion, making it less likely that he or she will ever feel comfortable in the stepfamily. A general sense of things not being quite right is felt; and in their imagination, children may develop a strong sense of being different, and may feel unable to be as carefree and happy as other children.

> "I hadn't noticed Darren was causing problems with the other kids at school until his teacher spoke to me. I was so tied up, what with the new baby, and his father is so busy at work." Mrs S.

Much of the pressure from these and other emotions comes from the fact that both adults and children are afraid to talk about their feelings. They prefer to suppress or deny them. It is always much easier to find excuses for the way we behave and there are so many people around on whom we can put the blame for the way we feel. It is also true that adults in stepfamilies may be unprepared for these strong emotions. Rather than face up to them they prefer to bury them. That means they never go away; they just fester under the surface.

Some people just cannot face up to the fact that their stepfamily is in trouble, because for many people in stepfamilies that would be an admission of just another failure to add to the previous failure.

"When Sandra comes back from seeing her Dad at weekends, she doesn't want to go to school on the Monday. I have to force her to go and she's nearly always in tears by the time we reach the school gates. It makes me so upset because normally she loves her school and teacher." Mrs F.

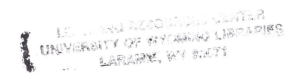

**CHAPTER 5**

# STEPFAMILIES AND THE FUTURE

More and more children will be brought up in some kind of stepfamily. It is critical that society should do all it can to help stepfamilies to feel accepted if they are to have a successful and happy future.

This book has focused on stepfamilies as a social issue and has perhaps given the impression that all stepfamilies must necessarily have quite awful problems. In fact, of course, stepfamilies can and often do provide a wholly satisfactory family unit within which adults and children can live happily.

Some of the problems mentioned in these pages are unique to the situation of stepfamilies, but many other problems arise from the powerful emotions of, for instance, jealousy and guilt, which are often present in relationships, but which can be increased by the stresses of stepfamily life. Stepfamilies also suffer from society's lack of acceptance of the stepfamily as a "normal" and respectable family type. Some of the problems stepfamilies face, then, can only be solved by society changing its attitudes and by revising its judgments. The legal framework within which the stepfamily operates, for instance, provides little support in times of difficulty. And yet a stepfamily is expected to behave as if it were a normal nuclear family type, taking on all the responsibilities of parents and family life. Only when more members of stepfamilies feel able to be open and admit to being in a stepfamily will they be able to feel at ease in our society.

In the United States, things have improved much more rapidly than in Britain: there is far less stigma attached to stepparenthood in the United States. Whether we like it or not, divorces are on the increase and so, therefore, are stepfamilies. And if second marriages are breaking up even faster – at the rate of one in two – then it is in society's interest to do all it can to encourage

stepfamilies to be successful. By making everyone much more aware of stepfamilies, by accepting them more readily as a large and rapidly growing family type, and by trying to understand the kinds of problems stepfamilies face, we can do much to help stepfamilies provide a more secure and self-confident framework for the full development of family life.

Doing things together – for instance on holiday – is important in building up a successful stepfamily life.

"When my oldest stepson got married I felt as proud as if I was his real mother. We'd been through so much together and I felt there was a part of me up there at the altar." Mrs J., speaking after Philip's wedding

# SOURCES OF HELP

If you would like to talk to someone about being in a stepfamily or to receive more information about stepfamilies contact:

**American Association for Marriages and Family Therapy**
*1000 Connecticut Avenue N.W. 1407*
*Washington, D. C. 10036*

Professional society of marriage and family therapists provides a nationwide referral service through this national office.

**Child Welfare League of America**
*440 First Street N.W.*
*Suite 310*
*Washington, D.C. 30001*

Write for referral in your area.

**Family Service America**
*333 7th Avenue*
*New York, N.Y. 10301*

Federation of 265 local agencies in over 200 communities which provide family counseling;

provides placement and computerized services.

**Help. Inc.**
*638 South Street*
*Philadelphia*
*Pennsylvania, 19147*
*(215) 546-7766*

Maintains a telephone counseling service and psychological and referral service.

**National Institute of Marriage and Family Relations**
*6116 Rolling Road*
*Springfield, VA 22152*
*(703) 2400*

Professionally staffed treatment, education and counseling centers that you can call to make an appointment or request a referral.

# WHAT THE WORDS MEAN

**access** refers to the legal right given to a parent to see his or her child after separation or divorce from the child's mother or father. A father, for instance, might be granted access to see his son every other weekend.

**cohabitation** occurs when partners live together without being married. They may or may not intend to marry, even if they have children. This kind of family is becoming increasingly common.

**extended family** is a term which refers to a family, common throughout the world in many other societies, where the boundaries of the family are not clear-cut. Ex-wives, ex-husbands, half-brothers and half-sisters, steprelations of all kinds – these form an extended family. Where a man can take more than one wife the extended family will be even more complex.

**nuclear family** is the type of family which is supposed to be the norm in our own society, and consists of a married couple with their own children. The boundaries to this kind of family are clear-cut. Most stepfamilies result from the breakup of a nuclear family.

**stepfamily** There are many different types of stepfamilies. Legally, a stepfamily involves only married couples, but it is usual to include all families where one or both adult partners bring one or more children from a previous relationship. Stepfamilies may be full-time or part-time. In a full-time stepfamily the stepchildren live with one natural or biological parent and the stepparent. In the part-time stepfamily the stepchildren visit the other natural or biological parent on access.

# INDEX

**Photographic Credits:**
Cover and pages 4, 6, 10, 14, 17, 19, 23, 27, 30, 33, 34, 35, 39, 40, 45 and 47: Topham Picture Library; pages 9, 37 and 56: Anthea Sieveking/Network Photographers; page 11: J. Allan Cash Library; pages 13, 21, 22, 25, 42, 49, 50, 59: Timothy Woodcock.